# CONTENTS

# MIGHTY BIKES

Motorcycles (or motorbikes, or just 'bikes') are vehicles with an engine and two wheels. Racing motorcycles and big touring motorcycles are mighty, high–speed machines that zoom by with a mighty roar.

Off-road motorcycle

Street bike

Sports bike

## TYPES OF MOTORCYCLE

There are many different types of motorcycle. Most motorcycles are for everyday road use, but there are also motorcycles that are built specially for sports such as track racing and cross-country racing. Although they do different jobs, all motorcycles have similar parts. Most motorcycles have two wheels, but some have three or even four.

Custom bike

● *Different types of motorcycle have specialised frames, engines, tyres and other parts.*

Leaning into bends is part of the fun of motorcycle riding. Riders enjoy leaning right over as they hurtle round a corner at high speed.

# LEANING OVER

Motorcycles fall over if the rider does not put his or her feet on the ground when the bike is not moving. When the bike is moving, even if slowly, it stays upright. When a bike goes round a corner the road pushes the tyres sideways, into the bend. The rider leans into the bend to counteract the push; otherwise, the bike would flip over. Some riders lean over so much, they almost touch the road.

**Tyres**
Rounded for leaning over

**Rider**
Leans over with bike

## FAST FACTS
**Staying Upright**
*When motorcycles are moving along, the spinning wheels work like gyroscopes. The spinning motion means that the wheels resist tipping over to one side.*

# HOW BIKES WORK

All motorcycles work in a similar way. The main part of a motorcycle is the frame. This is made from strong metal sections that are welded together. All the bike's parts are bolted to it.

## WHEELS, TYRES AND SUSPENSION

Motorcycles have lightweight, spoked wheels. The tyre tread is not flat like a car tyre, but rounded. This allows the tyre to grip the road when the bike leans over into corners. The wheels are attached to the frame by tough suspension springs that soak up bumps in the road, giving a smooth ride.

**Telescopic fork suspension**
Lets front wheel move up and down

**Swing arm suspension**
Lets rear wheel move up and down

A superbike with the body panels removed to show the frame and engine.

**Frame**
Supports other parts

**Engine**
Bolted to base of frame

**Disc brakes**
Give excellent stopping power

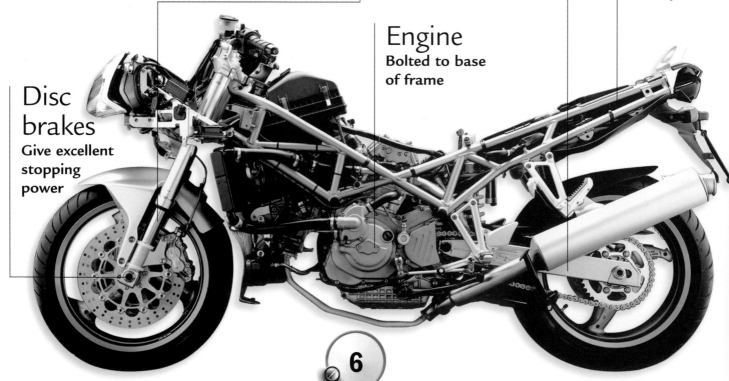

# MOTORCYCLE ENGINES

Motorcycles have two-stroke or four-stroke petrol engines. Engine sizes range from a tiny 50 cc in mopeds, to a giant 1800 cc – the same as a big car engine – in big touring bikes. Power from the engine goes to the motorcycle's wheels via a gearbox and a chain. A few bikes have a shaft drive instead of a chain.

**Valves**

**Drive belt to rear wheel**

◉ *A four-stroke motorcycle engine with two cylinders.*

**Gearbox**

**Cylinder**

**Piston**

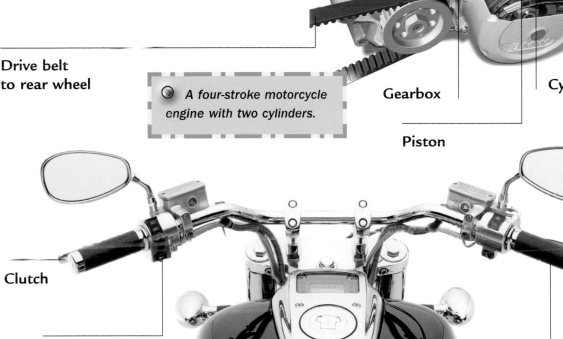

**Clutch**

**Horn button**

**Fuel supply valve**

**Front brake**

**Throttle**

**Rear brake pedal**

◉ *A driver's view of a motorcycle's controls. Gears and rear brakes are operated with foot pedals.*

## FAST FACTS
**Automatic Gears**
*Some bikes have semi-automatic gears. The rider changes a gear up or down by pressing a button on the handlebars.*

7

# EARLY BIKES

**The first motorcycles were built about a hundred and thirty years ago. They didn't look much like today's mighty machines. They were simply bicycles with engines.**

## STEAM AND PETROL

The very first motorcycles were bicycles with steam engines bolted to them to make them move. These hot, steaming machines were pretty dangerous to ride. The first motorcycle with a much safer petrol engine was built by German engineer Gottlieb Daimler in 1885. It was Daimler who developed the petrol engine.

### Stabilisers
One on each side to stop bike toppling

### Metal wheel rims
Protect wooden wheels

### Wooden frame
Supports engine and other parts

### Petrol engine
Drives rear wheel with a belt

*Daimler's motorcycle of 1885. Daimler's son rode 10 kilometres (6 miles) on the machine.*

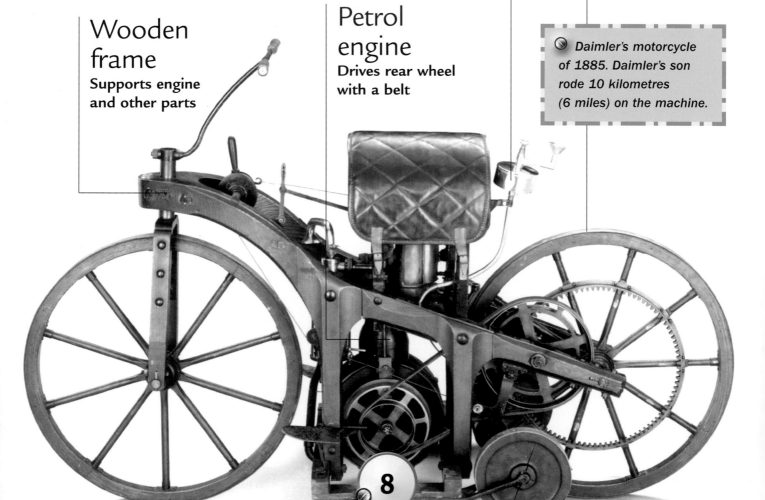

One of the first modern bikes was this Indian of 1905.

Single-cylinder engine

Fuel tank

The Rover Safety Bicycle was the first bicycle with a modern-style frame. Early motorcycles were based on this bicycle.

## FAST FACTS
### Pedal Power
*Early motorcycles had pedals for starting the engine and in case of engine failure.*

# THE MODERN LAYOUT

The makers of early motorcycles placed their engines in many different places on their machines – under the saddle, on the wheels, on the handlebars, and even on a separate trolley. In 1901, the Werner Brothers designed a bicycle with the engine at the bottom of the frame. All modern motorcycles have the same layout.

9

# CLASSIC BIKES

**Motorcycle enthusiasts collect the best and most famous motorcycles of the past. These are the classic motorcycles.**

1920s      1930s      1940s

## AMERICAN CLASSICS

Many classic motorcycles were made in the USA in the 1920s, 1930s and 1940s by manufacturers such as Harley-Davidson and Indian. Almost all had a big V-twin engine. Famous examples include the Indian Chief and the Harley Davidson 45.

### Fuel tank
Main tank and reserve tank

### Engine
With V-twin layout

**Indian Chief**
**Engine specification**

| | |
|---|---|
| When made | 1922–1953 |
| Engine | V-twin |
| Capacity | 1000 cc |
| Top speed | 145 kph (90 mph) |

The Brough Superior is a classic British bike. It was luxurious, very expensive and very fast!

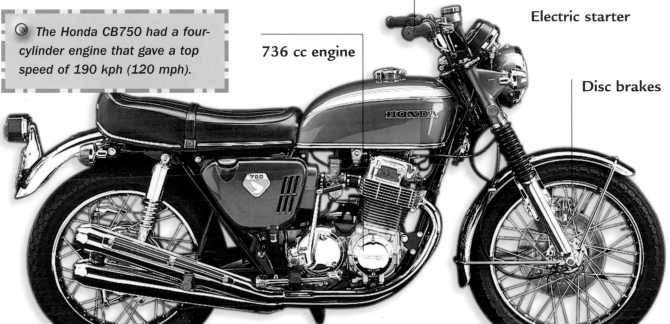

The Honda CB750 had a four-cylinder engine that gave a top speed of 190 kph (120 mph).

736 cc engine

Electric starter

Disc brakes

The big and powerful Indian Chief motorcycle was made from 1922 to 1953.

# JAPANESE CLASSICS

The USA and Britain built most of the classic motorcycles until the 1960s. Then, Japanese motorcycles arrived from manufacturers such as Honda, Kawasaki and Yamaha. One of the first Japanese classics was the Honda CB750, which experts think of as the first superbike.

## Paintwork
**Always red in colour**

### FAST FACTS
**Wartime Classic**
*More than 90,000 Harley-Davidson WLA motorcycles were used by the Allies during World War II.*

# SUPERBIKES

**The fastest, most powerful motorcycles are the superbikes. They have engines of 1000 cc or more.**

Suspension arm

Engine

Lightweight Wheels

## Honda CBR 1000RR

| | |
|---|---|
| Engine | four-cylinder in-line |
| Capacity | 998 cc |
| Weight | 180 kg |
| Top speed | 289 kph (180 mph) |

## STREET SUPERBIKES

Superbikes built to be legal for ordinary road use are the dream machines of motorcycle fans. They have the same technical features as racing bikes, giving them incredible acceleration and top speeds. The special features also make them safe to ride in the hands of experienced riders.

*The CBR 1000RR is Honda's top-of-the-range superbike.*

Frenchman Sebastien Gimbert racing his Yamaha YZF-R1 in the 2005 World Superbike Championship at Brands Hatch.

# RACING SUPERBIKES

Superbikes are also seen on the race track. They are raced in the World Superbike Championship and other championships around the world. These superbikes are stripped-down versions of street superbikes, with engine changes that give them extra power. They have better acceleration and faster speeds than the road-going bikes. They also have special racing features, such as slick tyres.

## FAST FACTS

### Power-to-weight

*A racing superbike engine outputs about 200 horsepower. That's about the same power as a sports car, such as an Audi TT. However, the bike weighs only one tenth of the car. The car would have no chance in a race!*

13

# BIG BIKES

**The mightiest motorcycles are built for cruising and touring. They are big enough to carry two people and their luggage.**

## CRUISERS

Cruisers are big, bold machines. They have the looks of classic, big American bikes such as the Indian Chief. They are long and low, with lots of shiny metal on show. Cruisers are for riders who want to be noticed. But these machines are not just for show. Big cruisers have lots of power when it is needed.

### Engine
Has six cylinders in two banks of three

### Radiator
For cooling engine

### Shaft drive
Carries power from engine to rear wheel

**Honda Valkyrie Rune**

| | |
|---|---|
| Engine | flat-6 |
| Capacity | 1832 cc |
| Weight | 360 kg |
| Top speed | 198 kph (123 mph) |

*This is the incredible Valkyrie Rune cruising motorcycle, built by Honda.*

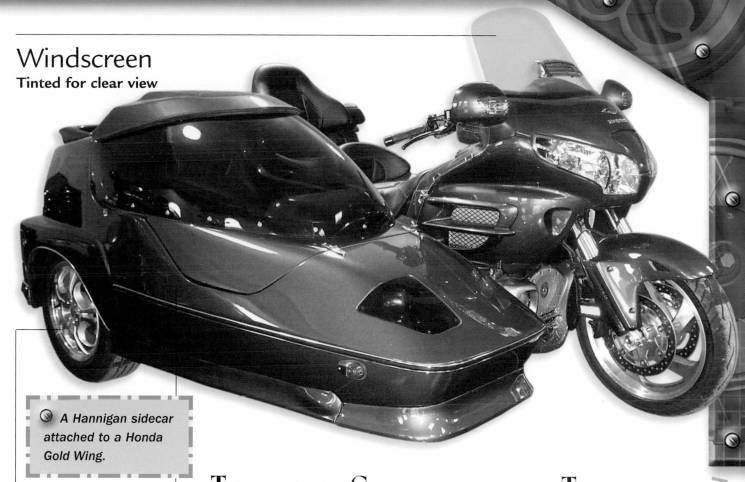

## Windscreen
**Tinted for clear view**

> A Hannigan sidecar attached to a Honda Gold Wing.

## Body
**Lightweight and aerodynamic**

## Third wheel
**Supports sidecar**

# TOURERS, SIDECARS AND TRAILERS

The biggest bikes are monster tourers such as the Honda Gold Wing and Harley Davidson Electra Glide. These machines are as heavy as small cars, but have engines many times more powerful. A sidecar can be bolted onto a tourer, giving space for a passenger and more luggage. Tourers can even pull small trailers.

### FAST FACTS

**No Leaning**

*A sidecar prevents a motorcycle from leaning over, so riders have to steer just with the front wheel.*

> Police forces use touring motorcycles for motorcycle patrols. The machines allow space for extra equipment such as spotlamps.

**15**

# TRACK BIKES

**Motorcycle riders compete on the track on many different types of machine, from superbikes to sidecars.**

## GRAND PRIX RACERS

Moto Grand Prix (MotoGP) is a popular worldwide racing championship. Bikes with the same engine size – from 125 cc to 990 cc – race against each other on the track. Strict rules on bike specifications make sure that no rider has an unfair advantage while competing.

**GP Superstar**
*Italian superstar Valentino Rossi is one of the world's greatest riders. He won the MotoGP title in 2005 on the 990-cc Yamaha YZF-M1.*

# SIDECAR RACING

A racing sidecar is a combination of a racing motorcycle and a sidecar. This makes a three-wheeled racing machine. An aerodynamic fairing covers the bike and the sidecar. The passenger is as important as the driver. He leans to one side or the other to stop the bike tipping up as it hurtles round corners on the race track at high speed.

## Passenger
**Leaning out to balance machine**

## Rider
**Controls the sidecar**

## Handhold
**For passenger to grab**

*A Formula 1 racing sidecar. It has a 1000-cc superbike engine.*

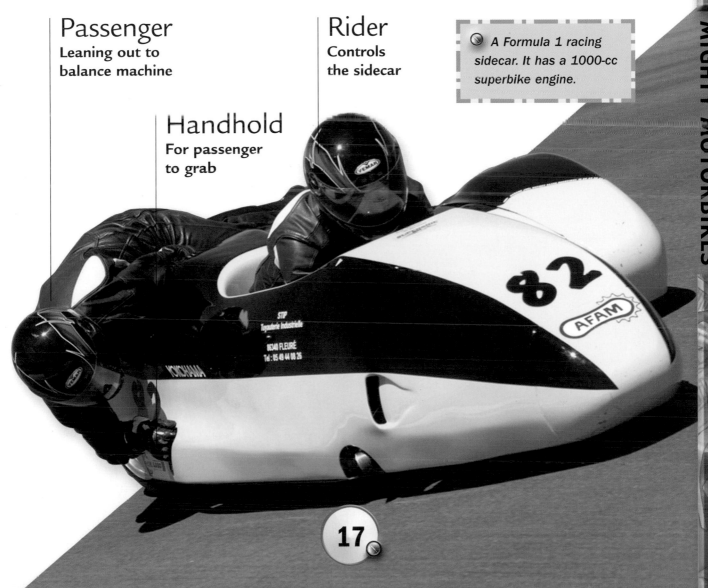

# OFF-ROAD BIKES

**Many motorcycles are designed for off-road use. They are used in motocross racing, for motorcycle trials, for rallying and for stunt riding.**

## OFF-ROAD FEATURES

Off-road bikes need special features to deal with muddy and rough terrain. Most important are tyres, wheels and suspensions. Tyres have a chunky tread to grip in the mud. Wheels are very strong, so they don't buckle after a jump. Suspensions are high to give clearance and to soak up the bumps.

### Engine
**Powerful to drive bike up steep hills**

### Suspension
**Holds bike clear of ground**

The Honda CRF450R is a powerful off-road motorcycle used in motocross racing.

### Skid plate
**Protects engine from rocks**

### Tyres
**Have chunky tread for grip**

Handlebar protectors

Riders often put their feet down to balance during a motocross race.

## FAST FACTS

**Longest Jump**

*The longest jump on a motorcycle is 84 metres, made by Trigger Gumm in Australia in 2005.*

A rider takes a corner on an ice speedway track.

# SPEEDWAY

Another type of off-road racing is speedway. The bikes race around a 400-metre oval track covered in dirt. The bikes have powerful engines, but no gears and brakes. Great skill is needed to slide the bikes sideways round the bends at each end of the track. A variation of speedway is ice racing, run on ice-covered tracks. For this, bikes are fitted with tyres with metal spikes sticking out.

**19**

# TRIKES AND QUADS

**Most motorcycles have two wheels, but some have three or four. Bikes with three wheels are called trikes and bikes with four wheels are called quads.**

A Triketec V2 Sport trike touring machine.

Rider's seat

Fuel tank

Car tyres

## THREE WHEELERS

Trikes have a single front wheel and two rear wheels. Having three wheels means that a trike rider can ride slowly and stop without having to put a foot down for balance. Trikes also have space for one or two passengers and luggage. They are becoming popular for cruising and touring.

Three-wheeled motorcycle rickshaws like this are used as taxis in many cities around the world.

| Bombardier DS650 X | |
|---|---|
| Engine | single cylinder |
| Capacity | 652 cc |
| Weight | 225 kg |
| Gears | 5 |

## Shock absorbers
**Filled with gas**

- The Bombardier DS650 X is designed for cross-country racing.

## Skid plate
**Protects bike from rocks**

## Foot plates
**Driver stands on them**

# QUADS

Quad bikes have a motorcycle engine, plus two front wheels and two rear wheels. Farmers use quad bikes to zoom around their farms, carrying supplies such as animal food and fence posts. The four wheels and chunky tyres give plenty of grip. Quad bikes are also called all-terrain vehicles (ATVs). These bikes have become popular as leisure and racing machines.

- Adventure riding in the desert on a quad bike.

## FAST FACTS
**Quad Adventure**

*Quad bikes are also designed for adventure riding in rough terrain, and for dirt-track racing.*

# CUSTOM BIKES

**Motorcycle enthusiasts often customise their bikes by adding new parts and artistic paintwork. They also strip away parts they don't want.**

## THE CHOPPER

Most custom bikes are called choppers. The name 'chopper' comes from the 1950s, when American motorcycle enthusiasts began removing or 'chopping' off unwanted parts of their Harley-Davidson bikes to make them lighter and so improve performance. Common features of choppers are long front forks, a low-slung rider's seat and a V-twin engine.

### Front forks
**Longer than standard bike**

### Front wheel
**On long forks**

This chopper is a customised Harley-Davidson.

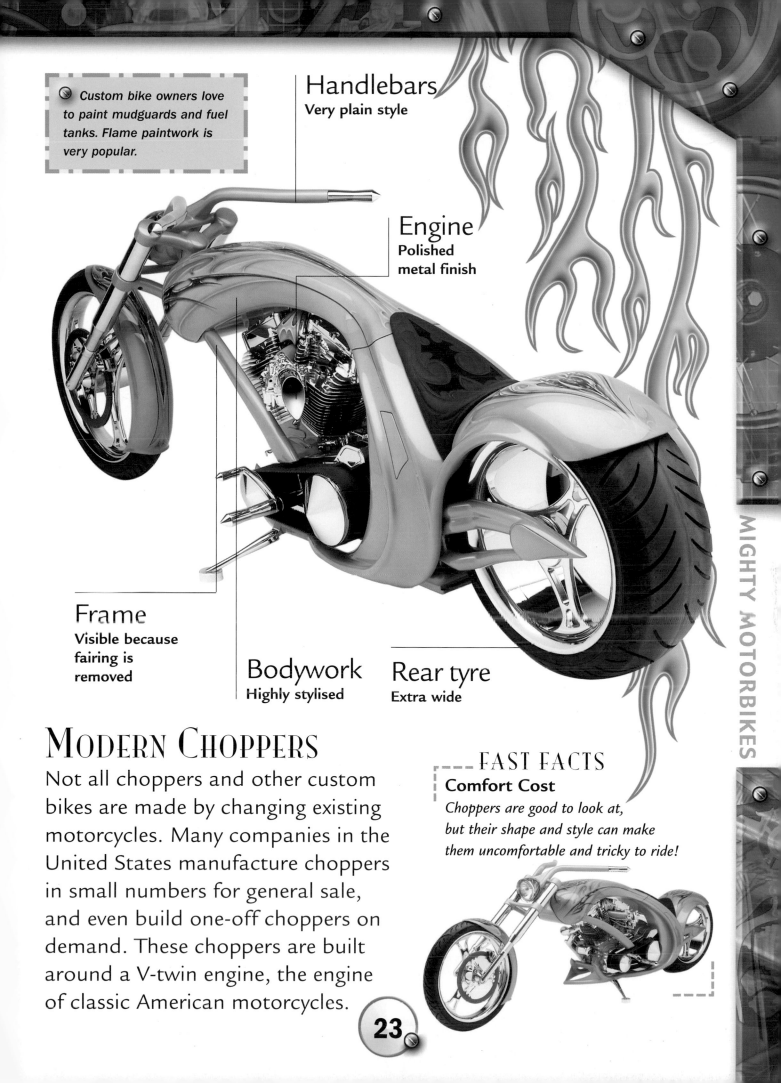

*Custom bike owners love to paint mudguards and fuel tanks. Flame paintwork is very popular.*

## Handlebars
**Very plain style**

## Engine
**Polished metal finish**

## Frame
**Visible because fairing is removed**

## Bodywork
**Highly stylised**

## Rear tyre
**Extra wide**

# MODERN CHOPPERS

Not all choppers and other custom bikes are made by changing existing motorcycles. Many companies in the United States manufacture choppers in small numbers for general sale, and even build one-off choppers on demand. These choppers are built around a V-twin engine, the engine of classic American motorcycles.

## FAST FACTS
**Comfort Cost**

*Choppers are good to look at, but their shape and style can make them uncomfortable and tricky to ride!*

23

# FAST AND FURIOUS

**Some of the most awesome bikes around have been built for eye-popping acceleration and terrific top speeds. They are the most powerful and fastest bikes on the planet.**

## SPEED RECORD HOLDERS

The world's fastest motorcycles are built specially to break speed records. These bikes are known as streamliners because the whole bike is covered with an aerodynamic body. These machines have many specialised parts as well as a motorcycle engine. Record speed attempts are made at the Bonneville Salt Flats in the USA.

**Fin**
**Keeps bike in a straight line**

*The Bub Streamliner has a 3-litre V-twin engine that develops a massive 485 horsepower.*

**Streamlined body**
**Made of carbon fibre**

**Engine**
**In space behind cockpit**

**Cockpit**
**Rider sits here**

**Solid tyres**
**Do not puncture**

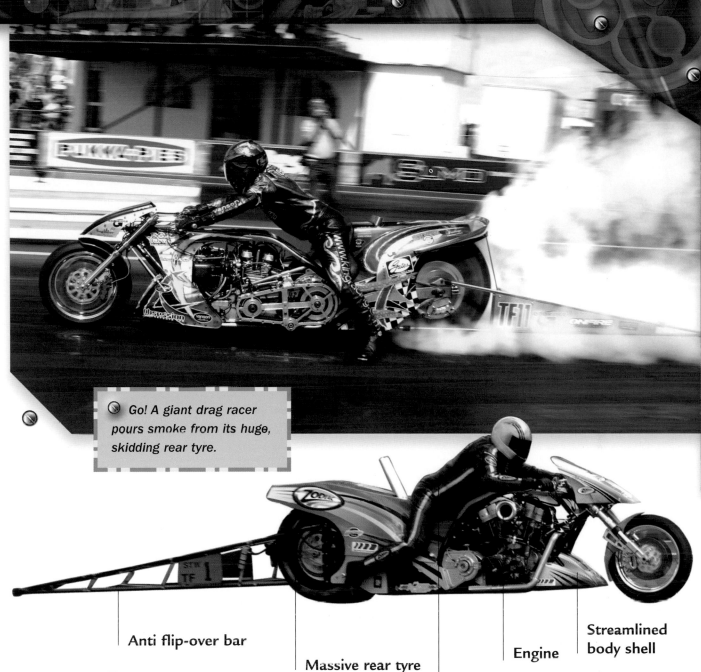

Go! A giant drag racer pours smoke from its huge, skidding rear tyre.

Anti flip-over bar

Massive rear tyre

Rider leans forward

Engine

Streamlined body shell

# DRAG RACERS

Drag-racing bikes are the most powerful of all bikes. The biggest drag bikes are giant machines with two, or even three, turbocharged engines linked together. They run on methanol or nitro-methane fuels, which give more power than petrol. The super-wide rear tyre provides all the grip needed to get the engine power to the track. Bikes race each other in pairs along a short track.

## FAST FACTS
**Fastest Bike**

*The current world speed record for motorcycles is 518 kph (324 mph). It was set in 1990 by the Easyriders streamliner, ridden by Dave Campos. The bike was powered by two Harley-Davidson V-twin engines.*

# BIG AND SMALL

**Motorcycles come in a bewildering range of shapes and sizes, but there are some extremely small bikes and some very big bikes!**

## THE BIGGEST

The world's tallest motorcycle is called Bigtoe. This giant bike is an amazing 2.3 metres high and 4.7 metres long. It is powered by a giant V12 engine borrowed from a Jaguar sports car. The bike needs stabilising wheels to stop it falling over. Music comes from four 500-watt speakers.

| Bigtoe | |
| --- | --- |
| Engine | v12 |
| Capacity | 6000 cc |
| Weight | 1,645 kg |
| Top speed | 100 kph (61 mph) |

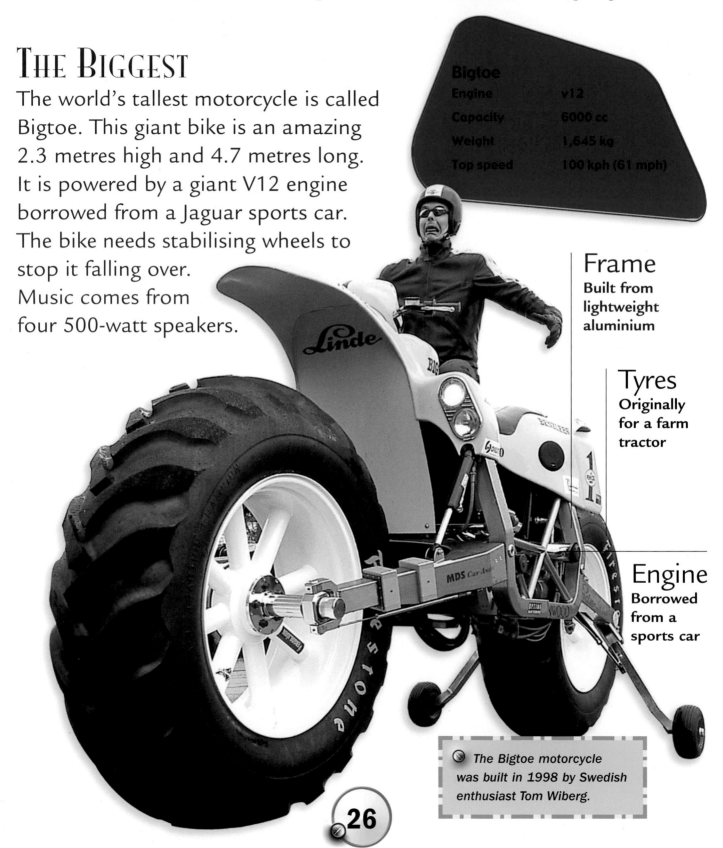

**Frame**
Built from lightweight aluminium

**Tyres**
Originally for a farm tractor

**Engine**
Borrowed from a sports car

The Bigtoe motorcycle was built in 1998 by Swedish enthusiast Tom Wiberg.

## Seat
**Large enough for adult rider**

## Handlebars
**With controls for riding**

## Body
**Perfect copy of real bike**

## Brakes
**It comes with disc brakes**

## Tyres
**Slick for racing**

A minimoto version of a track-racing superbike.

### FAST FACTS
**Tiny Cycle**

*The world's smallest motorcycle is just 6.5 cm high. It has a working engine and can be ridden!*

A minimoto race. The riders are braking into a corner.

# MINIMOTO

Minimoto bikes, also called pocket bikes, are tiny models of normal-sized bikes. They have all the features of the bigger bikes and are fully working. Minimoto bikes were originally designed for children to ride, but many adults ride them, too, and minimoto racing is now a popular adult sport.

27

# FUTURE BIKES

**So what will motorcycles of the future look like? And what new technology will future motorcycle manufacturers build into their machines?**

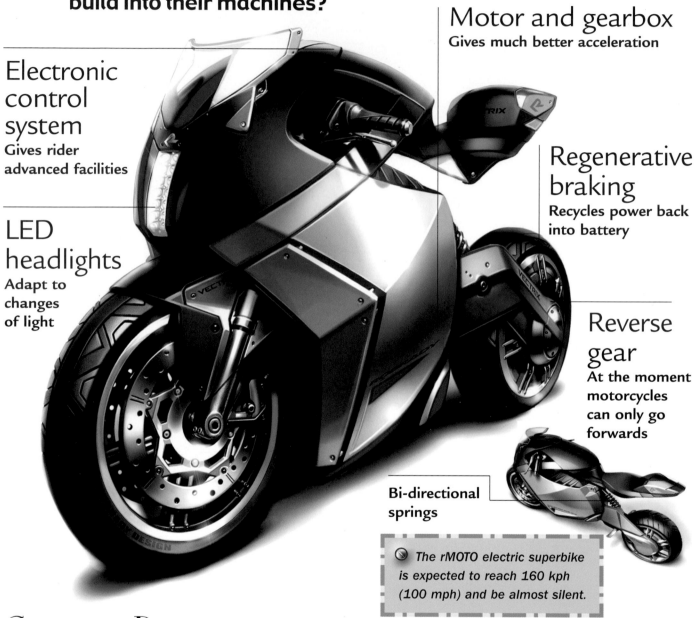

**Motor and gearbox**
Gives much better acceleration

**Electronic control system**
Gives rider advanced facilities

**Regenerative braking**
Recycles power back into battery

**LED headlights**
Adapt to changes of light

**Reverse gear**
At the moment motorcycles can only go forwards

**Bi-directional springs**

*The rMOTO electric superbike is expected to reach 160 kph (100 mph) and be almost silent.*

## CONCEPT BIKES

Concept bikes are visions of the future. When motorcycle manufacturers want to show off their latest technical ideas, they design a concept bike.

Some concept bikes are built to be shown at motorcycle shows. Very occasionally, a concept bike is actually manufactured and available for people to buy.

# NEW POWER

Motorcycles have been powered by petrol engines for more than a hundred years. The engines have become more efficient and less polluting, but they still work in the same way. However, there are now alternatives such as the fuel cell. This device produces electricity from fuels such as hydrogen, without any pollution. In a fuel-cell motorcycle the electricity works an electric motor.

**Sunshine Bikes**

*Researchers are also developing motorcycles that run on sunshine. Solar cells turn sunlight into electricity that is stored in a battery. The battery operates an electric motor.*

**Rear View**

**Top View**

*This fuel cell-powered bike can reach 80 kph (50 mph) and is almost silent.*

## Fuel cell
**Removed for refuelling**

## Controls
**Simple throttle and brakes**

## Electric motor
**Drives rear wheel**

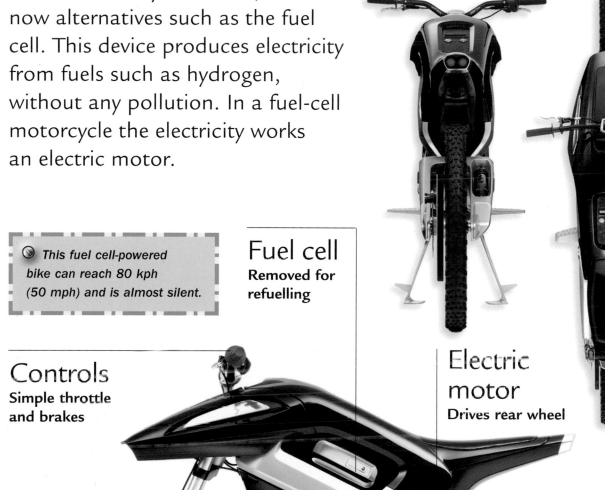

MIGHTY MOTORBIKES

29

# TIMELINE

## 1838
Scottish blacksmith Kirkpatrick Macmillan builds a bicycle with pedals.

## 1869
The first bicycle powered with a steam engine is built in France. It is the first motorcycle.

## 1885
In Britain, John Starley invents the first modern-style safety bicycle. It has a frame, chain drive and brakes.

## 1885
German engineer Gottlieb Daimler builds a motorcycle with a petrol engine.

## 1894
In Germany Hildebrand & Wolfmuller build the first production motorcycle.

## 1901
The French Werner brothers build a modern-style motorcycle with the engine at the base of the frame.

## 1903
The Harley-Davidson company is formed in the USA by William, Walter and Arthur Davidson, and William Harley.

## 1903
The motorcycle sidecar is invented.

## 1905
Motorcycles are fitted with a chain drive for the first time.

## 1909
Harley-Davidson introduces the V-twin engine.

## 1914
The first motorcycle trials race is run.

## 1920
Speedway racing is developed in the USA.

## 1922
Indian Motorcycle Company builds its first Indian Chief.

## 1935
The telescopic fork is introduced by the BMW company.

## 1939-45
In World War II, motorcycles are used by despatch riders and as machine-gun platforms.

## 1948
The Honda motorcycle company is formed in Japan.

## 1950
American bike enthusiasts build the first 'choppers'.

## 1968
The Honda CB750 is launched. It is the first motorcycle to be called a 'superbike'.

## 1974
American stunt rider Evel Knievel parachutes to safety after failing to jump a canyon on a trails motorcycle.

## 1975
The first Honda Gold Wing is manufactured.

## 1988
The first World Superbike Championship is held.

## 1990
The Easyriders streamliner sets the motorcycle world speed record.

## 1998
The world's tallest motorcycle, called Bigtoe, is built in Sweden by Tom Wiberg.

## 2005
Fuel-cell technology is introduced to the motorcycle world.

# GLOSSARY

## capacity
The volume inside the cylinders of a engine.

## cc
Short for cubic centimetre.

## chopper
Motorcycle stripped down to its bare parts.

## clutch
Device that connects or disconnects the engine and wheels.

## cylinder
A space inside an engine that a piston moves in and out of. Burning fuel pushes the piston out, making the engine work.

## exhaust
Pipes that carry waste gases from the engine into the air.

## fairing
Smooth cover over a motorcycle that allows air to flow smoothly over it.

## fork
Strut that supports a motorcycle's front wheel.

## gyroscope
A device for measuring or maintaining orientation.

## in-line
Engine arrangement in which the cylinders are arranged in a line.

## parallel twin
Engine arrangement in which two cylinders are next to each other.

## quad
Motorcycle or vehicle with four wheels.

## shaft drive
Spinning rod that carries power from a motorcycle's engine to its rear wheel.

## sidecar
Passenger compartment attached to the side of a motorcycle.

## single
Engine arrangement in which there is just one cylinder.

## slick tyre
A tyre with no tread, which gives maximum grip in the dry.

## superbike
Lightweight motorcycle with powerful engine and superb acceleration and top speed.

## suspension
System that connects a motorcycle's wheels and frame, allowing the wheels to move up and down over bumps.

## swing arm
Lever that supports the rear wheel of a motorcycle.

## throttle
Twisting handle that changes the amount of fuel reaching the engine. Used to accelerate or add power for going uphill.

## trike
Motorcycle with three wheels.

## turbocharger
A device that pumps air into an engine, allowing more fuel to be burned, and so improving power. It is powered by exhaust gases.

# INDEX

# WEBFINDER

http://www.motograndprix.com/en/motogp/index.htm  *Official site of MotoGP, with information on riders and teams.*

http://www.yamaha-racing.com  *Yamaha's site about their factory teams in all bike sport.*

http://www.bigdogmotorcycles.com/home.html  *Manufactures of classic chopper bikes.*

http://biphome.spray.se/bigtoe  *Photos, facts and figures about the world's biggest bike.*

http://www.bubent.com/racing/index.html  *Bub Streamliner photos and videos.*

http://powersports.honda.com/motorcycles  *Official site of Honda motorcycles.*

http://www.indianmotorcycle.com  *Indian motorcycles, including historical bikes.*

http://www.worldsbk.com  *Official site for World Superbikes, including track guide.*

# Mighty
# MOTORBIKES

## CHRIS OXLADE

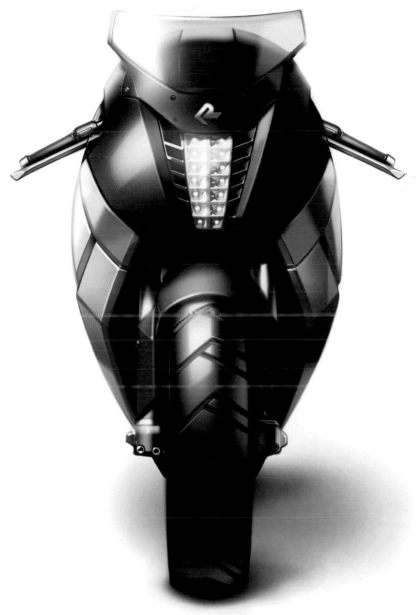

## W
## FRANKLIN WATTS
### LONDON • SYDNEY

 An Appleseed Editions book

First published in 2006 by Franklin Watts

Paperback edition 2008

Franklin Watts
338 Euston Road, London NW1 3BH

Franklin Watts Australia
Level 17/207 Kent St, Sydney, NSW 2000

© 2006 Appleseed Editions

Appleseed Editions Ltd
Well House, Friars Hill, Guestling, East Sussex TN35 4ET

Created by Q2A Creative
Editor: Chester Fisher
Designers: Mini Dhawan, Ashita Murgai
Picture Researcher: Deepti Baruah

ISBN 978 0 7496 7588 2

Dewey Classification: 629.227'5

A CIP catalogue for this book is available from the British Library.

Picture Credits
t=top b=bottom c=centre l=left r=right
BMW Group: 7t, Bombardier Recreational Products Inc: 21t, 21b,
Dave Jones/www.santapod.com: 25t, 25c, DIck Lague Ignition3: 24b, Doug Strange: 11t,
Ducati Motor Holding SpA: 6b, Gerry Walden/www.gwpics.com: 15b,
Intelligent Energy Holdings plc & Photographer: Ed Lee: 29t, 29b,
Jack Silverman/The Silverman Collection: 10-11b, Kim Kulish/Corbis: 27t, Michael Lichter / Michael Lichter
Photography: 23t, 23b, National Motor Museum/MPL: 8b, 9t, Q2A Solutions: 20b, Reno Anderson/
Hannigantrikes.com: 15t, STEVE COX & www.coxmx.com: 27b, ©Superside: 17b, Suzuki GB PLC: 5t, 19t, Goran
Svensson/Allt om MC: 26b, www.boonecountysports.com, Paul T. Zeien Jr. Photographer: 19b, www.hondanews.com:
7b, 11c, 12t, 12b, 14t, 14b, 18b, www.nmsi.ac.uk: 9b, www.rmoto.com/ & ROBRADY DESIGNS: Half Title, 28c,
www.Shutterstock.com: 22b, www.triketec.com: 20t, Yamaha Racing: 13t, 13b, 16t, 17t

Printed in Singapore

Franklin Watts is a division of Hachette Children's Books